Desperate for Dad

Desperate for Dad

Nicky Crabtree

SUNESIS MINISTRIES LTD

Desperate for Dad

Copyright © 2018 Nicky Crabtree. The right of Nicky Crabtree to be identified as author of this work has been asserted by her in accordance with the Copyright, Designs, and Patents Act 1988. All rights reserved. No part of this publication may be reproduced or transmitted in any form or by any means, electronic or mechanical, including photocopy, recording, or any information storage and retrieval system, without permission in writing from the author.

All of the characters in this book are fictional. Any similarity to persons alive or deceased is purely co-incidental.

ISBN 978-0-9956837-7-8

Published by Sunesis Ministries Ltd. For more information about Sunesis Ministries Ltd, please visit:

www.stuartpattico.com

The views expressed in this book are solely those of the author and do not necessarily reflect the views of the publisher, and the publisher hereby disclaims any responsibility for them.

Contents

Foreword	10
Born and Ready for Action	12
Learning the Ropes	16
Weekends with Dad	24
The Violin Years	29
Roger Over and Out!	32
Chubby Bunny	35
Another Hit	41
Life Goes On	45
Three in the Bed and the Little One Said	49
The Lonely Road	53
Choices Choices!	64
The Maze	68
The Turn Around	73

I dedicate this book to the one who is holding it in their hand. I wrote this book for you. My heart was to share my story with you in mind. We all have a story to tell and a journey to share and none of us are alone in that. My hope is that through my story you will find release, knowing that you are not alone and that there is another way. With love always!

A heartfelt account through the eyes of a young girl who is desperate for Dad Nicky takes us on a roller coaster of emotions; laughing, crying, cheering her on and feeling sad at the void she so much wants to have filled. There is a part of this girl in all of us. A poignant reminder that words matter and that real true love is not selfish but has to be given away if it is to have any positive affect.

Ange Pattico - Associate Leader at Joy Community Church

Nicky's voice couldn't be more relevant and necessary in this generation and the time we live in. She carries a unique gift and ability to reach those deemed by our society as `too difficult, unlovable or just too hard to reach. Nicky will stop for the one. Desperate for Dad will hit you where you're hurting and make you laugh at the same time but will also champion you right where you're at.  Her story is one of freedom and triumph, and rising above life`s circumstances whatever age you are. Today Nicky wears freedom like a coat of armour and I am immensely proud to call her friend.

Rose Graham- Officer of the court of The Ministry of Justice

A Story of childhood and searching for acceptance. A story of courage, bravery and resilience but above all a story of hope.

Zoe Bailey- Mummy of 3 and a graduate in social policy

Foreword

I didn't want to put this book down! I wanted to find out all about this young girl Nicky- I loved her straight away! I was so keen to know how she was going to overcome some of her challenges that life had thrown at her. Every page drew me in as she painted a visual picture of her life.

I love Nicky`s straight `from the heart` honest approach to her story, you really get a sense for her struggles and how she overcame them.

Having known my dear friend for well over a decade, I learnt so much about her in reading this book. Nicky has been brave in sharing her story. I have been encouraged to celebrate my life, even the hard bits because they are a part of me. Thank you Nicky, I look forward to hearing more of your story in future books.

As you read this book, be prepared to be challenged emotionally, be prepared to be sad, be prepared to laugh out loud, be prepared to mourn.

Be prepared to be wistful, to be angry but mostly be prepared to be filled with hope.

Elaine Simpson- Kingdom Choir Leader, Worship Leader and Songwriter

1

Born and Ready for Action

I was born in the summer of 1974 and according to my mum my birth was far from easy. It sounded to me a bit like a hokey cokey birth, but instead of my foot, it was my head that was doing the Hokey Cokey!

Mum said I just could not get out, she pushed and pushed but nothing was happening and I was dangerously stuck. Apparently the doctors became extremely concerned and at one point as Mum recalls it all became a bit worrying. She said that as the doctor turned around to wash his hands he was visibly anxious, then all of a sudden mum had a huge contraction and... whoosh!! I came flying out just in time for the doctor to turn around and catch me (I have always liked to make a grand entrance!) I'm sure if I could have talked I would have said "yes here I am world, I've arrived!" Not in a bolshie way, but in a wow I'm excited to be here way.

So there I was all born and ready for action. Well actually ready for milk, nappy changes and giving mum and dad sleepless nights but you know what I mean.

Mum always reminds me of the day I was born and has over the years repeated it many times. She'd say "I'll always remember when I held you in my arms in the hospital and you looked into my eyes and I said to you, " Well my beautiful girl I wonder what the Lord has in store for you?". I always pretend that I'm tired of hearing about it, but of course I love it really, "and your eyes" she'd go on to say "are exactly the same now as they were then!" and she would rock me and gently sing 'Black Pearl Precious Girl' over me.

Anyway back to the baby years.... So there I was all born and ready for life, obviously being newly born I don't remember much about the breast milk years, but much to my family's surprise I do have a good memory from my toddling days. I remember the colour of the inside of my pram and moving my head from side to side trying to get into a comfortable sleeping position and I would stare at the pattern on the inside of it, it was a really bold pattern in white and blue. I also remember where my cot was positioned in my room and distinctly remember screaming for someone when it was nap time. I also remember rocking and rubbing my feet on the cot sheets to get myself to sleep! (Still do it! Rub my feet on the sheets! Only rock though when I've had a really bad day..ha ha!)

So, moving onto toddler years.............

Mum recalls that I was a lovely chubby little ball when I was a toddler. You know the sort, little cuties who have dimples in their bums and legs because they're so chubby, and their little chunky arms look as though they're wearing permanent bracelets, (I have lost the bracelets but dimples won't seem to shift!! ha ha!)

I think I was around 18 months old and my memory, as I said, was good for some things that were great fun to remember. However some memories of mum and dad shouting at each other was not so fun, I can recall a time when I was in the sitting room. We had these, what seemed to me, like huge glass doors with a white rim that separated the room and they used to open or slide in the middle. I remember poking my face through them and watching mum and dad scream at each other! I felt totally confused, I knew it felt horrible but obviously being so young I didn`t really understand, however I do remember an overwhelming sinking feeling and sensing an anger and sadness in the air.

My next memory was living away from dad, with mum and my two sisters in a flat in Edgware over a salt beef bar and pizza place where we became a very tight but dysfunctional family unit. I adored my mum and sisters and still do of course, but in those days I started to love them in an "I'm responsible" for them kind of way.

So we settled into our new way of life and new routine quickly, as kids do. We were with mum during the week and saw dad some weekends.

I loved our flat; it was small but it felt safe, it had 3 bedrooms, a lounge/diner, kitchen, and a bathroom. We made it really cosy too with lamps and a snugly soft brown sofa that had a pouffe to stretch our legs onto. The lounge had a fire place with a mantel piece over it which had ornaments and pictures on, the dining table and chairs were near the window at the opposite end and we had an old brown finely tuned upright piano in the corner. It had a small kitchen with probably our 5th or 6th fish from the fair in a bowl in the corner.

It was home for us for a while and I loved it. I felt happy and secure there. When you came into the flats the main door was on a high street so we had to go up two flights of grey stone stairs. At the top we had a shute where we`d chuck all of our rubbish down in black bin bags which I just thought was fab! Apart from when our terrapin was accidently put down there but that`s another story!

All of the front doors at the time were painted a bright budgie yellow and we lived at number 15! It had a little step out the front where me and my sister would sit and eat our beloved beef flavoured monster munch, wearing our much loved roller skates. However I was growing fast and running out of play time as I was approaching that age and knew I had to get myself prepared and ready for the big one... SCHOOL!!!

There was a buzz of excitement at the thought of finally wearing that uniform that my sisters always got to wear and I didn`t. I had the shiniest black patent shoes on that I could almost see myself in. My uniform was navy blue; a smart white shirt with a blue and yellow tie and my hair was neatly put into bunches with a lovely straight parting. Photo`s had been taken and my whole family had pumped me up saying what a big girl I was now and how much I'll love school. The day finally came and I arrived at school with mum, my sisters had already gone in, mum took me to this long corridor where a teacher met us and mum handed me over, I held the teachers hand and was led away from mum. I remember I kept turning around to look at mum who was giving me encouraging waves, but she appeared to be getting smaller and smaller as we walked further and further down this extremely long corridor, tears started to burn my eyes as the realisation started to hit me that this school business might not be as fun as I'd been led to believe. That was my first ever memory of not feeling safe.

2

Learning the Ropes

Well School mmm!! To be honest I could have taken it or left it. It was okay but I just wanted to have fun, play and giggle instead of learn. I was happy at junior school and I liked the teachers however I always I thought I'd do a good job of teaching the class too. I was about 6 or 7 years old cheeky and bouncy. I loved to make people laugh I learned at a very early stage that humour was a great tool.

My school was Stanburn Lower School and it was a bus ride away from our flat, we had to catch the 186 from the bus stop over the road outside the flat. Mum would watch us from the window to make sure we were safely on. Fifteen pence each! How cheap was that! The girls and I would get safely onto the bus to go to school, waved off by mum from the flat window.

My nanny and poppa lived within walking distance of our school so sometimes we`d go there after, if mum was working. My nan was called Kitty short for Catherine and my poppa Billy, short for William. They were such warm characters. My nan was the sort of lady who was always dressed well, short set blonde hair always looked so nice and her make-up always done, bit of pink lipstick and rouged cheeks. She was always very smartly dressed and was often sucking an imperial mint. She`d be humming some sort of old fashioned song, or whistling this sort of funny windy whistle sound that wasn`t quite a full on whistle. She`d always have her leather gloves on in cold weather to drive her dark blue Hillman Imp car and do this sort of sharp ten to two style movement with the steering wheel! She was quite the nervous driver, and an even more, nervy passenger. Nan made wonderful cakes and always seemed to have a cut and come again cake on the ready for any unexpected visitors. To some, nan was quite a strong and controlling character the "I know best" kind of lady, but to me she was just my nan and I simply adored her.

Poppa was one of those people that everybody loved and people more often than not had kind words to say about him. He was a lovely round man with a lovely warm smile, always wore a smart shirt and tie with a tank top or jumper over the top. He was always smiling and when I say always, I mean always! He`d come home from his day and greet nan with his familiar whistle that he`d always do when he came through the door. Or when nan came home pops would greet her with the same whistle. He never had a bad word to say about anyone and always gave everyone the benefit of the doubt. If nan would ever go on to us about our fringe being in our eyes or not pronouncing our words correctly, Pop would always say "oh leave them alone Rodge" (which comes from my nans maiden name Rogers) I loved him for that. He had the best sense of humour. I'll always remember when I stayed with them overnight, which was quite often, and pops would make my favourite for tea, prawn cocktail! No-one makes me prawn cocktail the way my pops did. He would go out to the kitchen and me and nan would be snuggling up watching something on the TV, normally with a hot chocolate. He'd be out there for what seemed like forever,(especially when I'd be waiting and salivating thinking about my beloved prawn cocktail!!), then he'd come in, my little table all ready for me from the nest of tables they had, nice cold drink to go with, he'd have a tea towel draped over his right shoulder and place down his masterpiece....... of one small prawn a minute piece of cucumber, a seed or two of tomato and a crumb of bread!!! I'd do a double take at it and then look at him with a puzzled expression and he'd burst out laughing! We still do that trick to this day! Or if there was an evening of us all watching the TV and it was a sad programme and everyone was feeling a bit blue, Pops would leave the room and scoot upstairs. I used to think sad things were not his bag and he'd just leave the room but no not Pops, we'd all be sitting looking and feeling glum and fully absorbed in it when we'd hear him doing a "clearing his throat I'm back in the room" cough, only to turn around and he's standing there in nans bright red tights with a pair of socks shoved down the front doing his best plié! And with a rounded body and hairy muscley legs I can assure you it looked hilarious, and so we'd all laugh. He was just like that, he was at his happiest tootling around in the garden tending to his amazingly grown flowers trimming and pruning them. If I ever hurt myself he'd be there within seconds to check the wound or graze and find some sort of healing cream to minister or put a plaster on it. He'd always say "That's not too bad, not too bad at all, we can make that better". Pops was also a brilliant pianist; he played the piano as though his fingers were dancing along each key. He had a baby grand in the corner of the lounge and when he played, it would fill the whole house with that familiar sound of beautiful notes and chords all gathered together to create a known song. Nan would often accompany him by singing from the kitchen whilst finishing off the lamb

Learning the Ropes

stew that she'd been preparing all day.

Sometimes nan would fuss over silly things like our fringes being too long and in our eyes, or biting our nails, or whether or not we pronounced our words correctly, but I knew that was just her way. I remember nan would have us repeating` the rain in Spain stays mainly on the plane` or` how now brown cow` so that we would practice our vowel sound. I can see her now standing there saying `how now brrrrrrown cow` really rolling the r to, as she would say " get that mouth moving correctly". She was such a character and really as mum says should have been a professional actress! She always performed in the local panto`s and was brilliant at character parts. We were always surrounded with scripts and costumes so to see nan or mum for that matter in some sort of crazy costume was just normal everyday life for us.

So mum would come and collect me and it`d be home and bed ready for school the next day. I remember bits of lower school, some of the teachers, my friends and playing, mostly good memories, however I also remember having feelings of not quite being as good as everyone else. Not sure why, I just felt somewhat out of place, as though I didn`t really fit! The best part of my school day was always home time! I used to look forward to seeing mum so much and she`d always greet me with a big smile and a "How was your day?" As soon as I was near her I felt secure again. Me, mum and the girls would go home. I`d have to go upstairs to my room that I shared with my sister Linda to get changed, Nel had her own room at the time being the oldest she got first dibs.

Our room was quite small, we had bunk beds on the left against the wall with some outlandish retro yellow and brown duvet covers on (well it was the 70`s!!) we had cupboards on the right and a dressing table in between. My bunk was of course the bottom bunk being the youngest! I had my gorgeous first crush on a poster on my wall he was wearing his black shirt, bright bold pink jacket and standing on his toes doing his token move! Oh how I loved Shakin Stevens! Even dressed up as him to my own fancy dress party once!! I had a few cuddly toys on my bed and of course I had my very own......bogey collection! I know! Gross right!! But I have to be honest I was actually quite proud of it, that was until mum got so sick of it and made me wash if off and get rid of it. I know....over share!

I never really remember thinking of dad too much or feeling sad that we no longer lived all together, my security was definitely with my mum and my sisters. I had routine, I went to school, I knew mum would be waiting at the green gate or we'd walk to nanny and poppa's, Wednesday nights was fish and chips from the chippy over the high street and we'd eat it watching Star trek.

Weekends were either at home with mum or with dad. Life was okay, not great but okay. It was only as I grew much older that insecurities, low self worth and rejection started to take control and I started to believe the lie about myself, those `whispers` that I wasn't pretty enough, thin enough or clever enough and my life started to head down into a very dysfunctional direction.

Anyway back to the flat, so no more bogey collection, but still had Shaky rocking his moves on the poster on my wall. I liked spending time in my room and although my sister and I shared, we got on most of the time. We only had a few punch ups between the 3 of us, well mainly Nel throwing the punches, but apparently I was quite annoying. We were really close though and I think in those days we'd started to develop this survival coping mechanism of being really tough on the outside but screaming on the inside. My sisters and I became extremely protective of each other. Nel, my big sis was fast turning into the tough girl who got angry pretty quick at things soon after mum and dad split, she also started to take on the responsibility of being the other parent in the family, mainly fuelled by how much she loved me and Linda.

Linda however went from being bold and standing at the very top of the slide shouting to mum to watch her throw herself down, to very quiet and pulled right back on things, internalising her feelings and opinions. I became the caretaker and the in charge person (or so I thought!) I wanted to make everything alright again and make mum and my sisters happy. I would joke and mess about and try and make everyone laugh. I just thought at an early age that if I could make people laugh then they would stop being sad. I can recall one time in the flat mum was on the phone to dad she was standing in the hall with her head in her hand, they were arguing, that always made me anxious. She came off the phone put her head in both hands, slid down the wall and just sobbed. Me and the girls stood around her, I put my hand on her and had tears in my eyes and watched her sobbing. "Mummy are you o.k.?" I said. She`d say "Oh yes my darling I`m fine, don`t you worry" and she`d try and gather herself together to not upset us all, I remember my heart feeling as though it was being wrenched out of my chest when I saw my mum crying, I hated it and instantly wanted to make things better. "Well" I would say I am not writing this in my weekend news at school on Monday, that`s for sure!" and mum and the girls would all look at each other and laugh.

And so in my little thinking I started to realise that I could make things better by being a clown and making people laugh. When I saw my family`s tears turn into laughter I kind of felt better myself, and so I think from then on I became the clown caretaker of the family and then that became my taken on roll in life!

Being lots of girls in the house I definitely recall some hormone fuelled disagreements! My sisters and I laugh about it now but I recall a time when my sister Linda and I were in our room and seriously getting on each other's nerves.... mum was downstairs chatting on the phone and we were in our room arguing about a brush I think... I remember I wouldn't budge myself out of the way of the mirror and Linda was getting more and more annoyed with me! Our flat at the time was above a shop so we were quite high above the high street so it was quite a drop from our bedroom window. Anyway we continued to argue and shout at each other neither one of us giving in. I remember thinking right I've had it it's time to get physical ....she`d pushed as far as I was able to go...I turned to look in my cupboard in order to find something as heavy as I possibly could... in those days I used to wear clogs (I know! what a trend setter!) However they were super heavy! I grabbed that thing and I looked into my sisters eyes and held it behind my head... Linda looked at me and said "you wouldn't dare!" Big mistake! Not a good thing to say to me in those days! I lobbed that clog towards her head as hard as I possibly could, it hurtled towards her face...thank goodness she ducked just in time so the clog didn't hit her. However it did go flying through the bedroom window smashing the glass down onto the high street and the clog plunged down onto the ground!!

Our faces were a picture we just froze and stared at each other realising that we were now in serious trouble...and then we heard mums footsteps stomping up the stairs. She was understandably NOT BEST PLEASED! I remember this black bag we had over the window for what seemed like weeks afterwards to stop the draft coming in through the gap where the clog had smashed it, not a very proud moment.

Learning the Ropes

3

Weekends with Dad

My earliest memory of our weekends with dad was getting the train to his then pub in Putney called The 8 Bells! My dad ran it and lived there with his new wife Jenny and my step sisters Leyla and Miriam. Mum would say she would hate us going off for the weekend like 3 little packages! I used to like going on the train I thought that was exciting. Nel was always in charge and looked after Linda and me! Crazy really as Nel would have only been 13 years old herself!! I never really enjoyed being with my dad at the pub, I never really felt secure or wanted to be there! I always wanted dad to be like Charles Ingles from Little House on the Prairie! In fact I longed for my dad to be like him, he was so loving and protective of his girls on that show and I yearned for that!! I was a very affectionate child and loved to be cuddled and played with! I always felt with my own dad that he never really and truly loved me, I felt as though I was not really wanted by him. He would over the years say horrible comments about my mum in front of us or he would be angry about his life and how hard and unfair it was.

Weekends with Dad

I started to get angry with my dad from a very young age, I never verbalised it but I internalised and banked every bad word that came from his mouth and I stored it one on top of the other!! I used to use my clown acts and humour with dad because I thought if I made him laugh then that meant he liked me and I could be a part of his pride!!

Our weekends with dad were always in The 8 Bells and it was always a very drink centred way of living. I was oblivious to the drunken behaviour as I thought it was people just being happy and funny not realising in my childish understanding that my dad and his punters were more than often blathered.

One evening in the pub I walked past the bar and saw my dad crying behind the counter. It shocked me to see him like that, I'd never experienced him crying like that before so it stopped me in my tracks! I stared at him, then I asked him what the matter was, he just said that he wasn't crying in fact he was laughing and that someone had just told him a really funny joke! However I wasn't silly and I knew that he was sobbing.

That was the first time that I realised that my dad was really sad too! I hadn't really thought that before that day.

Lots of weekends with dad were pretty hazy with me only really remembering snippets of events. However I definitely remember Kew gardens.....we used to end up there quite a lot, and it was pretty boring if I'm honest! Flowers were not at the top of my exciting list at the age of 9! You've seen one you've kind of seen them all at that age! But it was free so I'm guessing that's why we went. We would walk around looking at the flowers and then looking at more flowers and then maybe a plant or four! However the exciting bit of the trip would be the burgers we used to have at the 'Inn' burger restaurant afterwards......I can honestly say they were the most delicious burgers that have ever graced my taste buds! All those years ago and I can still remember the smell and taste of those things! I would keep eating even though my stomach was full.....they were just too good to waste! That afternoon was good....a good memory! There was fun in the air, I recall us all having fun and dad was exceptionally jolly. We all climbed in to the car and we left headed for home when suddenly I had an overwhelming feeling of not being safe...Next thing I remember was a loud bang and the car suddenly stopped throwing me and my sisters into the back of the front seats. We'd had a massive crash with dad's car going straight through the front of someone's house! Turns out dad had lost control on a corner and was going too fast. Next thing I remember is this kind ambulance man checking me and my sisters over. He asked if I was hurt anywhere, I told him my head hurt.....dad quickly told the ambulance man that all was just fine and not to worry!!

Over the coming months my view of dad started to form and take root that I didn't really know him and that he didn't really want me.....I didn't really know him yet at the same time I was so in need of him! I would always visualize my daddy scooping me up into his arms and telling me how much he loved me and missed me when I wasn't with him...I'd dream of him telling me how extremely proud of me he was and that I was an amazing girl with a great future ahead of me. Sadly though that wasn't my reality and I was rapidly going into self protection mode. My mum became my angel and my security and my dad became the man who's only validation for me was that he didn't want me and that he didn't really love me....

We were travelling in the car one day and I recall my legs were not quite long enough to bend over the back of the car seat. They were just straight which to me means that I was young. Dad was driving and my sisters were with me too, Nel in the front and me and Linda in the back, I was looking out the window as we were going along and that's when all of my thoughts and feelings were stamped and confirmed.

I don't know if dad was just in one of his moods or not but the memory of the words he declared that day didn't leave me for an extremely long time!!

We were all chatting about something as we drove along in the car and as I remember the mood seemed good, when suddenly dad said to me "but you Nicola we never really wanted you, me and your mother only really ever wanted two children!"...BANG! And there it was; the shot that went straight through my heart. I vividly remember the feeling when it hit...I was shocked, I could not believe what my own father had just said to me. I looked out of the car window with my chest that had suddenly clammed up so tight that I felt as though I could hardly breath, my eyes started to sting as I held back my tears, my throat had a hard lump in it that made me feel as though I would not be able to swallow ever again. My sister Linda was sitting in the back with me, she stared at me to see if I was ok, the atmosphere in the car had changed drastically and I could almost feel both of my sisters feeling mad and hurt for me, but we all said nothing .The silence that filled that car was so apparent. The lie had shot me through my heart and rejection was now fully activated within me, my very own father had declared it so it had to be true. I was not meant to be here, I was unwanted by my father, he not only told me but he had stamped it with a confirmation that day.

I often think of that well known saying "sticks and stones will break your bones but names will never hurt you!"......RUBBISH! Word`s are powerful, they can build a person up or knock a person down in an instant, they have power! That day, at that young age I was knocked out and those very words pierced my soul and stayed with me, feeding that monster of rejection that followed on for a very long time.

However life continued as it does and I continued on, back home with mum and my sisters and of course back to school. I did seem to bounce back after such a day and as children do I carried on being my cheeky little self! We were all in routine at school and I had even started to enjoy it there a little bit even though the nose picking had continued and I think even the teachers were getting fed up with the nose bleeds. I honestly don't know why I used to do it....it could have been boredom in class, my mind did often wonder and I never really grasped why we were doing certain tasks, but I would always look as though I knew exactly what I was doing and what was going on which leads me beautifully in to the violin years!

The Violin Years

I was the kind of child that would see someone do something amazing and think to myself......I can do that! Whether it was tumbling gymnasts or a talented musician, I would watch people and work out in seconds, how they held themselves, their facial expressions, their timing, how they walked, how they talked etc.

I remember being at nan and pops one day and we were watching a programme about young musicians when on the screen came this beautiful little Chinese girl with the shiniest hair and the most cutesy face. She walked on in front of the orchestra so confident and bold! She positioned herself ready to begin and as she started playing, I was mesmerised! As she flicked her shiny hair around whilst her tiny fingers danced up and down the neck of her violin, the sound she produced was so beautiful. Then when she finished the audience went crazy clapping and cheering for her. She smiled sweetly, curtseyed, thanked her orchestra and slowly, walked off the stage. "That is it" I said to myself, "That's what I can do......I can do that!!"

I obviously hadn't taken into consideration "all" the preparation and practicing and dedication it had taken that girl to get to that event of playing on the television! Nevertheless off I went thinking.... I can do that... I too will play the violin like that and I am going to swing my hair whilst my fingers dance up and down the neck of my violin exactly the same. I too will do that wiggly fingered thing to make my notes sound nice. That's it I thought to myself, I have found my thing... can't wait to get started!

I was focused. My brand new violin was bought. My pops would be my orchestra and I was ready for my first practice, duster placed over my shoulder, hair freshly washed ready for the swing! Resin applied to my bow, hands in position, Pops ready at the piano. I was ready to meet my destiny and I, Nicky, would start my journey towards a possible duet with my hair swinging friend!!

That was until the bow touched the strings of my violin! I looked very much like my Chinese friend I was positioned beautifully and focused but let's just say a sudden realisation came over me that I may have a little work and fine tuning ahead of me. I'm not sure if the sound I actually produced with that thing had 'ever' been heard before but I can definitely say that it was extremely 'unique'. Nevertheless I had a plan to conquer the world with this violin and so I scraped on. My pops would very patiently accompany me as I would scratch out each note next to him. In fact I do recall the first and one and only time during our practices that my pops ever got angry with me. We were there in the lounge... I was ready to play standing by pops who was sitting at the piano encouraging me with each note and reminding me about my timing, I was looking at my fingers whilst playing each note, desperately trying to get it right as I played the tune I was getting more and more carried away with my bowing getting more and more vigorous with that thing. When all of a sudden I poked the end of the bow right into the side of my poppas right ear! It must have really hurt him as he shouted! "Nicola....you must be careful with where you are going with the end of your bow", He was rubbing his ear and his face went red! I remember being ever so sorry and explained that I was looking at my fingers and must have got too close to the side of his head. I sheepishly carried on practising and he continued to accompany me. (What patience!)

The day arrived for my first exam. Mum drove me to a house and spoke words of encouragement as we travelled, as she always did. She would always remind us to say a prayer and tell me we were never alone as Jesus would be with me! I remember feeling so scared... I had never had an exam for anything before so I didn't know what to expect! I met with the lady who would examine me at her door and she let me into this, what smelt like a dusty old musician's room! I had to play my piece and do a sight reading piece. I passed, but not with flying colours. I came out, got in the car and said to Mum " well Jesus was definitely with me, but He must have gone for His tea when I did my sight reading piece because that did not go well...at all!"

5

Roger Over and Out!

He crept into my room, it was dark and I was sound asleep in my bottom bunk. He gently woke me up, cradled me in his arms, he seemed sad! He rocked me and kissed my cheek whispering "Goodbye Nicky, I'll miss you"

"Goodbye" I said, I'll see you in the morning". "No" he said "I have to go, I won't be here again".

That was the last time I ever heard his voice. I remember feeling so confused and sad. He was going to be the Charles Ingles daddy I always wanted.

Roger was my mum's partner for a while and I had grown to love him a lot. He was funny and made me laugh a lot. He would play with me and tell me stories. He had long hair and a beard, he wore glasses with tinted lenses and dressed in garish funky clothes, I don't remember exactly how long he and mum were together but I know it was long enough for us to form a bond. He loved me. He would always pick me up or push me in my buggy.

One of my fondest memories was after dinner one day. We were all sitting at the table as we always did and pudding came out. It was jelly and Roger taught me and my sisters a new way of eating it by pushing it through our front teeth and squidging it around our mouths! We thought that was great and all had a go at mastering it. Another good memory was when we all stayed out at a friend's one night and I was on a pull out bed. It must have been winter time as when I climbed into the sheets they were really cold. I called for Roger who came in and said "That`s easy, you get into bed and wiggle your legs and body as fast as you can and it warms it up! I always do that" he declared. So I wiggled my little legs and body around the bed as fast as I could and hay presto my problem was solved.

Roger would tell me stories and listen to me when I wanted to talk. He would put me on his shoulders whenever we were out and about and when we played I'd ride on his back like a horse! I simply loved him and he became a very important part of my little world. When I was with him I had that child like feeling that everything was going to be okay now because he was going to be our new daddy and look after my mum and sisters and me! I was no longer rejected; he really cared not like my real daddy.

I was very young and although my mum gave us so much love I so longed for that father figure in my life and was sure that Roger was going to be just that. However I was wrong and I didn't see that my mum and Rogers relationship was on thin ice and eventually Roger had to go.

That was the night he came into my room to say his goodbyes! And as I said earlier that was the last time I ever heard his voice. The last time I ever saw him was one morning when I was waiting at the bus stop for the 186 to take us to school. It was a very profound moment in my life that stayed with me for a long time, and I still remember it like it was yesterday. I was standing in my school uniform and sucking my thumb looking at the traffic as it passed by. I looked to my left and saw a small white transit van that I slowly recognised to be Rogers, my heart started to beat with a sense of excitement. I remember vividly thinking that he had come for back for me and a wave of adrenaline rushed through me. It was Roger! The van slowed down and I saw him sitting in the passenger seat, he saw me, I was so excited, he gestured to me to take my thumb out and stop sucking it as he always did when he was with us! And then the van with him in it just drove past and away into the distance. I felt crushed. He didn't stop. He didn't stop. I stood and watched the back of the van as it disappeared into the traffic. Why didn't he stop I thought to myself? I went to school with an overwhelming feeling of sadness followed by a small voice deep inside my head that said "He didn't stop because you were not worth stopping for, he never really loved you".

6

Chubby Bunny

Chubby Bunny! I love the name of this chapter it not only makes me smile and chuckle to myself but it brings back the memory of that day when my heart and soul was filled with the most amazing love and acceptance that I had ever experienced in the whole of my life. I didn't even fully understand it at the time but I knew I had done something that day that was one of the best decisions I had ever made in the whole of my life.

My mum always raised me to know a truth... that Jesus loved me. I was young when I first heard those words so I didn't fully understand about this man named Jesus, but I had this love and warmth towards Him. I felt like I already loved him and knew Him well.

My mum and sisters were due to go away for a break and mum had booked us all to go to Spring Harvest which was in Wales. I was excited. I loved long journeys as I got to sing all my most favourite Shakin Stevens songs and play games with my sisters, Like when I went on holiday and took an item then we had to remember the previous item and add our own and so on and so forth. I was so looking forward to spending time with mum and both my sisters. My sister Linda would get so annoyed with me when I sung any Shaky songs especially one in particular " Green door". At the end of one of the lyrics Shaky would sing and sort of flick up his note at the end of the word' door' in the song and of course I would try and mimic that, as I knew it got right on my sister's nerves I used to do it more but start from the very beginning again just to wind things up again, however would normally only manage a few more flick of the notes before I would get a sharp elbow jammed into my ribs.

I'd always get "Nicky if you're going to sing then get the words right and sing in tune at least!"

Anyway we were all packed up and ready to go, bags in. Us three girls all

squished into the back like three little sardines. Why one of us didn't sit in the front I don't know! Ah yes I do recall now. My mum had only gone and invited one of my School teachers to come on the trip with us!!! AWKWARD! Mum had asked Miss Fry if she wanted to come on holiday with us and what was worse, she only came!!!

How bizarre and weird I felt with my teacher being in the front of my car with my family coming on my holiday. What was my mum thinking! Had she gone mad, didn't she know that now I'd have to be on my best behaviour all week!! ARGHHH.

However having brushed my bruised self down and put my embarrassment to one side, took in a large intake of breath and started my second Shaky song!

After what felt like an eternity finally we arrived; we all jumped out of the car and stretched, soon after we found the chalet we would be staying in and ran to claim our beds.

Camp was good fun, we'd all meet up and play games and get to know the other children. We would sing songs and listen to stories but mostly I remember the atmosphere was really nice. After the day came to an end and all the events were over we all headed back to our chalet. It suddenly dawned on me about who was going to sleep where, as I would not want to be sharing a room with Miss Fry....no WAY! I sat in the living room and counted up; there are five people and only two bedrooms......five people and only two bedrooms!! There was one room with bunk beds and a single bed in and one room with a double bed in. Mmm I thought, I know for sure that my mum won't be sharing a bed with my teacher so that only means one thing! I'm going to have to share a room with my teacher! Mum....what were you thinking, I thought to myself again!

Anyway having no choice I got on with it as it was time for bed. I was on the bottom bunk, Nel on top and Miss Fry in the single bed. My bed was really comfy. I wiggled my legs to warm it up. The room was quiet, a lovely dusky light was soaking through the curtains, I was really warm and just about to drop off to sleep, when it started!!....THE COUGH! It was one of those coughs that started off quite gently to begin with but then it got worse and worse and worse! Why on earth wouldn't you bring some sort of linctus or lozenger with you if you knew you had a cough like that at night!

So quick recap, mum invites none other than my school teacher away on holiday with us, travelling ALL the way to Wales and me having to be on my best behaviour, not easy!, and not only that but having to share a room with her and the cream on top... with a cough that would prevent someone with narcolepsy from falling asleep!! If I ever needed Jesus, it was that weekend, and I haven't even shared about the pillow incident yet!

It was night time and we had all come back from another day at camp, Nel and I were in bed already and we had started to argue about who's turn it was next time to sleep in with mum on the next night! I fought my corner hard as I was desperate to have a night away from "the cougher" especially as I could almost feel the calm air and a quiet night's sleep that I would have, snuggled up to my mum. I wasn't about to give that up easily!

"I`m sleeping with mum tomorrow"

"NO.I.AM" I'd say

"No....I am!" Nel would reply, getting more and more aggressive,

"Am"

"Not"

"Am"

"Not, you spoilt little brat" Nel would say, we were in a full on shouting match, neither of us would back down. I knew I was on thin ice as Nel in those days would seriously lose it and me and Linda would often be on the end of her loss of control. I still did not back down. I was fighting for that sleep next to mum! The argument continued but Nel had had enough. The room we were in was quite sparse and there was not a lot for her to grab and smack me with, however, she had a pillow in her hands and she suddenly came toward me with a look of absolute intent on her face. Ow sugar I thought, I`m dead!! Next thing it was over my head and I could almost taste it. I vividly remember thinking help! My sisters going to kill me, I tried to shout but couldn't get any noise out as it was pressing too much against my face. I tried to wiggle and fight her off but couldn't breathe. Nel had seen red so she was in a full on rage! I started to see dots in front of my eyes and I knew that was not a good sign! Suddenly she took the pillow off of my head and I could take a full breath again. I was breathing heavily grateful that I was actually conscious. I looked at Nel's face she had an utter look of shock across it as if she had realised what could have just happened! She looked at me, moved forward again and I flinched. She wasn't going to do anything else, and she scooped me up and hugged me. I think she was nearly crying at how she had lost control and how far she had taken it. Me...I was just grateful for a lot of air that was filling my lungs back up again, and was thinking I'll be able to talk in a minute and get the last one in "I`m sleeping with mum tonight!!" but it had truly affected Nel and she looked into my eyes and said "I`m so sorry Nic, I didn`t mean to do that, lets pray together"

"Pray!! Are you having a complete laugh! You just tried to kill me with a pillow!!" I declared!

Anyway I did get to sleep with mum the next night but Mum however had no idea what I had gone through to claim my victory spot next to her.

The next morning the sun shone through the chalet curtains, it was bright and warm and there was a buzz of something special in the air. It was the children`s fun day and I was really looking forward to having some fun and games. We were all gathered in a large tent, there was a really nice feel in the air. I sat in the front row where there was a man chatting to us. Then he asked for three volunteers to come up to the stage. I was intrigued as on the stage was three chairs and three buckets in front of the chairs. I threw my hand up into the air, I locked eyes with the man willing him to choose me, he did, "Yes" I thought to myself. We were going to play a game called `Chubby Bunny`. I sat on the chair giggling with excitement. We had to take a marsh mellow and put it into our mouth and say "chubby bunny", then we had to put another one, and another one, and so on! We all looked like little hamsters with packed cheeks! The words chubby bunny was getting harder and harder to say! I had what felt like 400 marsh mallows in my mouth but I wouldn't give up. I wanted to win as I knew you would get a prize! However after the fourth or fifth marsh mallow I had to give in. The boy that was sitting next to me had won. Everybody clapped and laughed as he was given his prize of a huge bag of none other than marsh mallows!

I sat back into my place with everyone else and listened to the man as he continued to tell us fun stories and jokes! Then he started to talk about Jesus and how much He loved us, he said that no matter what we had done in our lives, where we were from or what we looked like, that Jesus loves and cares about us. Mum had talked about Jesus a little bit and we had prayed together before but there was something amazing about how I felt sitting listening to the man that was speaking. My tummy started to feel warm and my heart started to beat harder, as though I was being called by someone I was so excited to see and hadn't seen for a really long time! I felt safe and in familiar territory, I felt as though I was the only child in the room and the man was only talking to me. I remember thinking...I want this, I want Jesus! The man said to us all "If any of you would like Jesus Christ to come in to your hearts today, raise your hand". I raised my hand and stood up to walk to the front. We all said a prayer and we were given a booklet. I walked away feeling as though a warmth had just entered my entire body and I felt like crying. I was eight years old. (I truly believe that making that decision on that day saved my life more than a few times growing up).

Our time at Spring Harvest had come to an end and we all travelled home the next morning, I gazed out of the window all the way home with my face covered in a huge smile. We said goodbye to Miss Fry and all went home to the flat together.

7

Another Hit

Smelling the daises, playing with worms, running through crunchy autumn leaves, being cheeky and giggling at girly things, singing shaky songs, rolling on skates to my friends as fast as I could to see her new gerbils but remembering not to be late home as it was Wednesday and star trek and fish and chips was the order of the night.

That was me, a little girl that was happy and grateful for the simple things in life, I had this new glow in my heart from Spring Harvest and I felt alive and free. The one small problem I had was still there and it was deep within me, locked in a part of my soul where it needed it to be kept until I was able to understand and know that it wasn't my fault. I was scared and confused, and the worst thing of all was that it was still happening to me.

Sometimes when we saw dad at weekends we would visit grandpa and grandma's house. We would often see our auntie, uncle and cousins there too. I loved getting together and playing with my cousins. We always had fun and enjoyed lots of different games together. Grandpa and grandma lived in a large house with a large well kept garden! Nothing really to play with but we would make use of the space we had to run around in. There would always be the familiar smell of beef casserole roaming through the house. We had some Christmas celebrations there and some fireworks nights. I remember the indoor fireworks would always be at the table and we would all have to keep really still and not get too close as we watched the fireworks sparkle and flame into different colours! We would watch old Sony films on the white wall in the lounge of us all when we were little, running around in the garden with grandpa and grandma, lovely memories mostly.

I don`t remember the exact time the abuse started but I vividly remember the day I realized that something was totally wrong.

We had all had lunch and decided to go to the park for a walk and to play on the roundabout and slide. It was a very windy day and the trees were shedding their leaves, so I'm guessing it must have been around autumn time. I remember the satisfying sensation of the leaves crunching under my feet. It must have been pretty cold still as I was wearing gloves to keep my hands warm. Grandpa wanted to hold my hand; I remember he was holding it so tightly that I felt incredibly uncomfortable. I tried to let go but he just held it even tighter almost hurting it. Eventually we arrived at the park and he let go of my hand. I remember it like it was yesterday, the overwhelming feeling of total relief. I ran into the park as fast as I could, the wind vigorously blowing through my curly hair. I ran and ran looking up at the trees, they were moving in the wind, almost as though they were looking and talking to me, I felt free! That was the moment I realised that what grandpa had been doing to me was so terribly wrong, it was like an aftershock rumbling through my body.

I started to feel uneasy when I was ever near him. I didn't fully understand but I was frightened. I felt so uncomfortable and on edge whenever I was with him, he was no longer safe to me, he was someone I was no longer comfortable near.

I started to become aware that the tickling game was often the start of the abuse. As a child I loved to play and be thrown around and be tickled like all children do but it was when things changed during that game that I remember well. I can only describe it as a fear that gripped every part of me, a shock that almost stopped my heart. I would freeze and almost stay locked in the moment in time because that was all I could cope with. I couldn't shout or think about my mum as I normally would if I ever I felt I was in danger. I couldn't even make a sound. I was caught in a state of trauma. I just coped with it. I remember being more terrified of my manic beating heart bursting through my chest. It was pumping so hard that I could hear it in my ears.

It carried on, it seemed to me to get more and more frequent. I had never experienced fear like that, the way my chest would clam up and tighten so much that it felt like it would snap.

One of the worst times was when I was taken out of my bed. I was fast asleep one night and had a feeling of being lifted which woke me up into a sleepy haze! I can remember being held under what seemed like huge arm and I couldn't move. The fear had come over me once again but covered in a hazy sleepy mist, however I couldn't misunderstand that familiar feeling of my heart beating so fast that it would almost jump out of chest. All I could hear was my heart beating in my head once again... boom...boom....boom!   Then the silence would become so incredibly loud, I was actually frozen with fear, I had never experienced that before.

I was totally confused and really afraid, I wanted to tell someone but I was scared that I would get into trouble. I said nothing for a while until I built up the courage to tell my cousin.

We were playing in the bedroom at grandma and grandpas house on the floor by the bed in the spare room. I asked her "Has grandpa ever done anything to you before?" She looked at me with a puzzled look on her face so I went into a bit more detail. She looked at me now with a shocked look on her face "no" she said, and continued to say that she was going to tell I had said that! I was really scared of getting into trouble so I quickly claimed that I had made it all up and that I was only joking! That message to me was that I must not ever tell as I was the one who would be in trouble. I carried on carrying it alone! Year's later grandpa suddenly died one morning whilst walking to collect the paper. I was relieved that it had stopped but I was sad at the same time. My grandfather was gone but my secret was still very much in me and alive! I had no choice but to carry the weight of that all by myself.

8

Life Goes On

It was late afternoon and I was snuggled up on our sofa watching Little House on the Prairie. I was absorbed in it. Charles Ingles would come home on his wagon; his wife would wait at the door for him with a huge smile across her face, his dark curly hair and tanned skin, his high cheek bones and chiselled looks! (Not dissimilar to my own dads features at that time). He would jump from his wagon greet his wife with a hug and a kiss and then as quick as anything ask where his girls were! They would rush down the stairs shouting Daddy! Daddy!..at that point in the programme tears would nearly always start to sting my eyes. I used to try as hard as I could to stop it happening but I never quite managed it! It was always that programme that got me, it was the way he was with his girls he just loved them and they were so important to him, and he was a real daddy. I craved that love and nurturing that I saw on the screen. How fortunate were those girls to have that sort of love and protection from a daddy that they had. I hungered for that. I was desperate for that protection and guidance that he was a brilliant example of. That programme always made me realize that that was so absent in my own life. I had made Charles Ingles the dad that I was hoping for; that was exactly how a father should be in my mind that was my expectation. I knew that I had a hole in my heart and a gap in my soul and it seemed to be expanding with life's events and happenings that I was experiencing.

However like other people in life we carried on and continued to grow. My sisters and I continued to do each day as it came, we would roller skate up and down outside the flat, go to the shops to buy our beef flavoured monster munch, we would knock for our neighbours, play games, make up more dances to our favourite songs and so on and so forth.

School was still a puzzling experience for me. I went in every day and took my cheeky self to each class. I was always confused about what we were doing and why, but being young I thought it was just my age and that I would grow out of it at some stage. I always felt really different from all of my friends and other students, they all seemed to grasp the task set and be able to get the work done! I spent my time looking at other students work in order to keep up! I was able to do creative things really easily. I really enjoyed those subjects, but as time went on in my school life I started to be more and more concerned about whether I was liked or not, or who I could make laugh to gain their acceptance! I liked people, all people. I didn't ever care about back grounds like some kids did. I liked the cool kids and I liked the not so cool kids! The only people I couldn't be kind to were bullies! It would make me so mad to think that someone could be unkind to someone just for fun! I simply never got that concept ever!! (I found out later in my school life what it was like to be on the end of that nasty behaviour!)

So my routine continued on, go to school, meet my mum at the green gate after school (best part of my school day!!) If mum wasn't able to pick us up I knew I would go to my nan and pops house (greeted with a drink and a slice of cut and come again cake). Wednesdays nights was Star trek and fish and chips, Shaky was my pin up and my future husband. My sisters and mum were my whole world and we went to see dad some weekends!

I don't remember the first time I met my mum's new boyfriend! But I do remember how tall he was when I used to look at him. He seemed huge to me definitely from giant heritage of some sort. He was 6ft 4inch tall with dark hair he had dark green/brown eyes with a very softly spoken voice! I used to think it was funny that he wore a silver belcher necklace with a door key on the end of it! And he wore clothes that always looked worked in.

We used to have parties at the flat sometimes, they were fun! Friends and family would come over for drinks and laughs and break out into songs accompanied by guitars! My mum's new boyfriend would come too so we all got more familiar with each other. I was quiet around him at first which for me was quite a different response! I would normally have jumped on him straight away and asked him a million questions about him marrying my Mummy but I think maybe because of Roger being gone I was slower in coming forward with my 'normal' way.

His name was Will. The first time he came over to our flat officially was when mum had invited him over for a chicken dinner.

We were all sitting around the table as we always did for tea, only this time there was a giant at the table, he was sitting next to me. We were all eating in silence which was unheard of at our normal banquet!! There was a tension in the air as we all ate, me and my sisters were doing our side glares at him and then knowing looks at each other afterwards! I would steal a quick glance at Phil again then look at my mum who was being as upbeat as she possibly could! I remember looking at my sisters to gauge how to behave and get confirmation of how to act as I often did! But they were eating in silence too. mum was starting to look a bit uncomfortable when all of sudden the giant said "well I don't think much of this chicken!" and he threw the chicken leg over his right shoulder into the lounge in a bid to break the ice and make us all laugh and prove to us that he wasn't all that scary really. Well, our eyes came out on stalks! We would NEVER have been allowed to throw our food on any occasion! We were all amazed that mum didn't go ballistic but then found it really funny and all burst out laughing! It went down as a really good memory and it certainly did break the ice and confirm that he was ok!

9

Three in the Bed and the Little One Said

It amazes me that with some of us in life, parts of our past memories or chunks of our lives can simply go missing or just cannot be recalled!

We lived in our flat for 8 years of my life but I remember absolutely nothing about moving out! I don`t even remember packing my room, talking about moving out, nothing at all! I was 10 years old. Was I happy about the move; excited; sad; disappointed? I can`t recall a single memory about it. Maybe I blocked it! Maybe I didn't really want to move from what I saw as my secure safe haven! After all it was routine for me and it felt safe in our little flat!

However the move was inevitable and we moved into Will's bungalow until the house sale went through! "It will only be for a few weeks" we were told! Again, I don`t remember the actual moment we moved in or how I felt when we first walked through the door of our new, but ` temporary digs`.

Will had the most beautiful golden retriever called Georgie. She was such a lovely natured dog with a lovely friendly face. She was so gentle and her tail would always wag as we approached her.

The bungalow was really well decorated. The lounge had really posh sofas in it, they were orange and brown with dark wood surround! Definitely not kid friendly! The dining area was open planned and led onto the kitchen; everything was decorated to a really high standard! The bathroom was amazing...it was tiled from the floor to the ceiling with multicoloured green tiles there was imperial soaps by the basin and the bath!

The garden was a good size, certainly enough for Georgie to run around in and the four cats to mooch and slomp about. There was of course only one problem!! Only two bedrooms! WHAT! Hang on I thought....um....three kids and two bedrooms, obviously with three growing girls there must be three beds right!! As I looked in the spare room I couldn't see 3 beds, but I could see one very small pull out sofa bed! "Are you having a laugh" I said "IVE GOT TO SLEEP WITH BOTH OF MY SISTERS.....IN ONE SMALL BED"!!

"It won't be for long" Mum kept reassuring us. That`s it.... I was in trauma; did they understand how this was going to be for me?! Obviously being the youngest I would have the in the middle of them both option! Well, that's me not sleeping for the unforeseeable future I thought to myself!

Nel used to sleep like a giraffe that was just coming round after being sedated for a while and Linda used to sleep like princess and the pea but if you wiggled or even breathed to heavily she`d get the royal hump and tell you to be quiet! I certainly would not be allowed to snore or dribble! Anyway, muggings was sandwiched in the middle night after night next to the giraffe and the princess too scared to move in case I got a kick or moaned at.

However we got with it and mum would keep reminding us

that it wouldn't be for long and it was only until we could move into our new house! We were looking for a house in Watford at the time but one had fallen through so our time at the posh bungalow went on much longer than we had all originally expected.

I don't remember seeing dad much whilst we were staying there! I think our visits with him were starting to become few and far between which is all too familiar nowadays with some family set ups!

There were strict rules in the bungalow; no nail varnish in the lounge that was for the bathroom! No legs up and slumping over the sofas etc, I remember feeling quite aware about how I was expected to behave and I think I started to feel incredibly restricted and a little bit on edge! I didn't feel as though I could relax fully. I was more than aware that we were living in Will's home and I was old enough to realise that I should respect that, but I wasn't really happy there.

The summer holidays were coming to an end and we were all due to start our new school at the beginning of September! It was pretty tough for both of my sisters as they had to go into years that were already established groups of friends, but I was ok as I was starting year 5 so everyone was new. Linda found it tough and understandably pretty upset on her first day, She'd left some really good friends behind and wasn't keen at all on moving to a new school.

Nel was away with my dad on holiday for the first week of the new term so she would probably be even more glared at when she arrived! To be honest, I didn't make it any easier for her as I had told lots of people that my big sister was a model and a complete hard nut who wouldn't be taking any rubbish off anyone. When Nel heard what I had done and said, let's just say she was not best pleased with me. She couldn't believe how I had paved the way for her arrival at her new school. Oops!

I on the other hand settled in pretty quickly, I made friends with these three girls who were all really nice. We started to become really good friends. I was finally really happy at school......for a while anyway!

10

The Lonely Road

I had this love hate relationship with school and learning. I loved the social side of school but did not enjoy the learning side of things. I found it was all very confusing to be honest! My brain would seem to only allow a certain amount of information into it and then went into overload mode, it simply shutdown which would trigger me to become the `mess around girl` in class. That was the cycle I seemed to take at school with the learning side of things anyway. Humour was my main tool whenever I felt inadequate or scared about anything. Making friends came quite easily to me, but in those days I thought I had to earn a friendship or prove to people I was worthy of being liked, I didn't really care who liked me as long as I was liked and accepted.

The thing that kept a spring in my step at that time was that my gorgeous little brother had arrived into our lives, he was such a cutie and a true blessing, he had big brown eyes and a little fluffy head and I simply adored him. He was always good to get home for and I thought about him a lot when I was at school.

I carried on plodding through school with, what was at the

time, an unknown learning difficulty. I knew that I didn't progress as much as others seemed to be progressing, and I copied whoever was sitting next to me to get by and try and mask my lack of understanding. I remember always feeling like the underdog or the thick one at school. My character was big but in so many ways I felt so misunderstood. I felt as though I had this pot of gold shining in me but absolutely no one saw its brightness!

In the classes I felt so out of place; things would be explained to me but it never seemed to stay in my head, it was as though I had a leaking valve somewhere in it. Sometimes I would do all of my work and put my absolute heart and soul into it and be super proud of myself, only to realize that I had got totally the wrong end of the stick of the task set or I had focused on totally the wrong part of a question given. I would feel deflated and have to deal with sniggers from more academic pupils, other times I'd put my hand up in class eagerly to answer a question feeling excited that I actually had an answer for once, the teacher would say "yes Nicola" I'd answer and the teacher would tell me off for not listening properly to what we were being asked or I was told to stop messing around! Deflated was the feeling I got used to at school, not being understood. I was actually really trying and crying out on the inside, but like my light not being seen my silent voice was not being heard.

My solution to all of this was to start acting as though I didn't care. I became the class clown but with the underlying need of being liked and accepted by my fellow pupils and my teachers. I was in conflict with myself with what was going on, on the inside of me and the outside of me!

My school reports were always firm but fair; lack of concentration was the general running message all of the teachers gave, except in drama where I was always an A+ student! "A lovely girl but must concentrate more" or "doesn't always understand the tasks set!" I remember English especially I had no concept of punctuation, where it was meant to be placed or why. I knew question marks, they were easy but commas and full stops always threw me! If a teacher explained about paragraphs or semi colons or spelling long words it was like a totally different language to me. Although I really tried to grasp it, it just didn't settle into my brain at all. Eventually the inevitable happened; I started to shut down on learning. My mind set was totally wrong and I told myself that I was obviously thick and I was never going to understand all this information the teachers were teaching me. So back around the mountain I would go, really trying, shutting down, being the class clown, and being vacant back to really trying and back round the mountain I would go.

In most lessons, I would rely on other pupils to help me or just secretly copy their work and try to put it into my own words. My writing was always pretty neat and my artwork was always really good so I guess I was much more creative than I ever was academic. However I carried on "coping" in school self worth was starting to take a nose dive and I was always fiercely comparing myself to other girls.

I had a lot of friends in school. I got on well with both boys and girls. Boys I always found less complicated! I mostly hung out with three girls. Nat was a tall, slim pretty girl with beautiful dark skin and she was really gentle in her ways and always really encouraging. We were the closest I think. Then there was Ray; she had curly blonde hair, naturally cute looking, small frame and a small mole under her lip, she was shorter than me and Nat. Then there was Helen; she was quite plain looking but had the best pair of legs in the year with gorgeous olive skin that always looked flawless to me. We would giggle at silly things and we had our little sayings that made us feel connected to each other.

I'd go around to the girls houses outside of school to make up dances to Madonna songs and have midnight feasts if I stayed over! Those were good memories and really happy days for me, we would talk about boys and who fancies who, and chat about when we're all older wondering what we'd do and who we'd marry, fond memories!

I was around 13 or 14 years old when thing took a sudden turn. Girls seemed to suddenly turn on you for no particular reason. I remember going into a class as normal one morning and the atmosphere between me and my three friends seemed really different. I tried to sit down at the chair but one of the girls pulled it in as if to say you are not sitting here! I was shocked, I racked my brain to think of something I may have done or said to upset them! I couldn't think of anything! I sat in the class with this panic in me searching myself for what had brought this all on. I couldn't even hear what the teacher was saying I was mortified.

Things changed drastically for me from that day. It was as though a missile had been shot at me and I had to deal with the debris of what was left behind! The girls just cut me off. I was out in the cold, out of the clique, their sudden change in behaviour let me know that I had officially been booted out of the pack. There was no "hi" in the mornings anymore, just cold and dirty looks.

I hoped it would only last a few days and it would all blow over but it didn't, in fact it got worse. The ignoring and dirty looks I could pretend didn't really bother me but it was when a few weeks later the hard nut group decided to jump on the bandwagon was when I knew things were getting more serious! I had to think quickly of a new coping mechanism! I played every possible scenario in my head that I thought may happen and I practiced how I would respond to every eventuality!

The hard nut group of girls I used to get on ok with, they were known as the tough girls with really scary older sisters! One of the girls had boxer sized hands that were huge. They all had curly hair with over sized flicks at the front and they always wore the latest trainers and the cool clothes. They always spoke quite aggressively and thrived on how tough they all were often using intimidation! Girls that I wouldn`t want to get on the wrong side of however I now was and they quickly formed an alliance against "Nicola" and things got a lot tougher over the next weeks.

I started to get shoulder budges and whisperings followed by over the top laughter and stares followed by sarcastic comments! Most days for me became about trying to avoid them all. I didn't really have many friends to hang around with, apart from one girl, Maggie, who thought this whole vendetta against me was ridiculous so she remained friends with me. I loved her for that, even to this day I never forgot that act of kindness. Life at school really started to affect me and I started to withdraw not only out of school but out of life! It all became too much for me to cope with and I was getting really low. Living with the constant dread and fear created a state of anxiety in me. In class I would sit with someone I didn't know or I would sit on my own, I was feeling extremely isolated and lonely. I remember looking at the teachers in class and silently screaming at them "don`t you see" I WAS SO DESPERATE! I would will them to notice how unhappy I was, but no one saw and so it continued. Eventually the bullies tried to get what felt like as many people on the `hate Nicola campaign` as they could! It was me against loads of girls, even the hard nut girl's sisters got involved and all her croons! I didn't know how to make it all stop, I felt more and more out of control and I didn't know how to make it all stop. I followed the boy I was dating around at lunch times and breaks in order to get some protection, but he soon got fed up with me being needy and decided to dump me, I think that was nearly the last straw.

I had got to the point of nearly giving up. I could not see any way out of this misery. I didn't feel safe at school. I didn't feel comfortable at home. I felt misunderstood and disconnected from life. I had got into a desperate place in my mind. My thoughts were being bombarded with how to get out and how to make all this fear and pain go away. My thoughts were heading towards getting out of life, heading towards the only thing I could think that would make it all go away. I thought if I was dead I would not only be free but it would also punish every one of those girls for being such bullies to me. I would gain some control back and have the final say then they would have to live with the fact that they made me so unhappy that I had taken my own life because of them. The seed was in. I even felt a bit better for having a plan of my own.

I sat in the upstairs bathroom of our new house; I was sitting on the floor staring at a glass and the tablets I had placed by the sink. Thoughts were rushing through my head of the feeling of freedom and revenge. This is the answer to all my problems I thought. I stared at them both for what felt like hours, when suddenly I was ripped out of my trance by my mum opening the bathroom door. She stood and looked at me then looked at the bottle of pills and water on the side. I looked at her and we stood there for a minute, neither of us quite knowing what to say or do, "Nic what are you doing?" she said. I just shrugged and looked at her with tears in my eyes but no words available. After that I just carried on as though nothing had happened and I just presumed my mum thought I was just having a teenage moment.

The summer holidays arrived and I welcomed them with open arms, the freedom from school with a feeling of relief was overwhelming at times. I was away from that constant pressure, the feeling of having to survive each day with not understanding and trying to act brave and strong whenever I bumped into the bullies!

I always found things to do during the summer holidays. I'd be much happier that was until about week 5 of the 6 weeks as that's normally when I started to mentally prepare for going back.

July and August seem to fly by and September was now looming towards me and I knew I had no option but to get ready to step back into the Lion's Den again.

The morning arrived when we had to go back to school. I was dressed in a new outfit that mum had bought me, an attempt at making me feel a bit better about going back and feeling better about myself. I was wearing a crisp new white shirt accompanied by the usual tie we all had to wear, a long grey stretchy skirt that were all in at the time, bright white socks with slip on black shoes and a new leather look jacket. I actually felt good about myself. I felt if I looked nice and felt good then things might just change the situation at school and maybe the girls will want to just drop everything and be friends again!

We all shuffled into our form rooms. There was a buzz of excitement in the air and lots of pupils wearing their new uniforms all ready for a fresh term and a fresh start. I had a little glimmer of hope that this term will be different and the torment would end. The day went slowly and I was changing classes to go to my second lesson when I bumped into one of the bullies, I tried to smile at her willing her to smile back at me but she didn't. She budged past me laughing and sniggering making fun of my `fake` leather jacket, saying she can't even afford real leather. I was deflated to say the least. I knew then that things had not changed and I was still in exactly the same position as before the holidays. I was deflated! I went into the familiar survival mode techniques I had learnt like trying not to bump into them during break, go really quiet in classes, try and look as though I wasn't scared of them, act as though I didn't care, try and make myself invisible around school. However with all of this going on in my head I still had that small voice in me that said I had to keep going and I had to hang in there.

School went on and so did I. I would hang around with my lovely friend Maggie who had decided not to get on the "bully bandwagon" and stick by me. If Maggie was not around I would normally sit on my own or look for one of my sisters to be near them. It was one lunch time when things really peaked. I could almost sense the atmosphere change and the air smelt different, I felt unnerved, I noticed to the left hand side of the upper playground a gaggle of about 6 or 7 girls all huddled together talking and laughing, like they were scheming something and against someone. They all stopped as I walked past and gave me the death stare. I remember looking at them with their over the top blue eyeliner and crispy hair do`s. They were wearing tight black leather jackets and long tight pencil skirts. My stomach was in knots and I instinctively went in to flight mode. I had sensed correctly, they were going to get me! The bullies sisters were on board and they were bad news and known for fighting. My heart started to beat faster and my cheeks were turning red, my first thought was get to one of my sisters. I started to run. I ran around the corner away from the top play ground which was higher than the lower play ground towards the smooth light coloured building at the side which was the P.E block to see if I could see Nel or Linda there. I burst through the red double doors, but my sisters were not there so I ran to the music block where I finally spotted Nel standing with her friends! Thank goodness I remember thinking! Nell will deal with them, with my panic filled voice I explained to her what was happening and asked her to help me. However help didn't come in the way I wanted it! I was kind of hoping she would say "Right I'm going to sort these girls once and for all" but it didn't quite happen like that. She said "right Nic go up to all of those girls and tell them you'll take them all on!" WAS SHE MAD!!....Did she not like the way my face was placed?! And did she realise exactly what she was saying? I admit I didn't think much of myself in those days but I was quite fond of my rounded head shape and didn't really want it changed! I didn't choose that suggestion; instead I just ran around the school hiding until the bell rang. I made it safely onto my next lesson with my face and head all intact!

That was the day I must have gone home and finally spoken to my mum about how horrible my day was and how I had escaped being beaten up. My mum must have had enough too as unbeknown to me she went into the school to fight my corner and get things out in the open in order to sort out a meeting with me and the girls involved. The next day I was called into the office where the three original girls were already sitting, I went in nervously and sat down. We were told to talk things through. However I could tell straight away that things were the same, there was no remorse and they had absolutely no intention of inviting peace into the situation. The conversation was clipped and there were lots of sideway glances between them. The hierarchy had clearly not given any kind of instruction to give the go ahead for reconciliation as yet. So nothing had changed and I plodded on with my coping mechanisms.

I can't remember how long things continued to be tough for but I do clear as crystal remember the day things started to improve. I was in my worst lesson, geography, it was a warm day and we all had our jumpers off with flush cheeks, we were being taught by a lady teacher who used to shout a lot!

I had shut down in her lessons a long time before this particular day and was often pulled up by her for not listening or not concentrating well enough! My mind set in those days towards learning was not good and I had told myself I didn't need geography and if I ever needed to get anywhere when I'm older I would just get myself a map, so really didn't see the point in the lesson!

Like I said I had shut down! I was getting increasingly bored and started to look around the class, my eyes settled on the back of one the bullies' heads, and I started to wonder how I could make her laugh. I looked at the teacher and it clicked. My teacher at the time had a very large nose and was well known for it in the school (I know! Kids can be so mean) however I wasn't being directly unkind to upset the teacher I just really wanted to make the girl in my class laugh who was part of the unkind gang! I quietly bent forward trying not to disturb the class or make too much noise, under the desk I rolled up a piece of paper to make it look as much a a nose shape as I could , I found something to stick it on with and sat there quietly with a large nose shaped piece of paper stuck to my face, I glared at the girls head willing her to turn around and look at me not even considering that my teacher would see me, I was so intent on using humour to put an end to all this pain, when suddenly "NICOLA!!" she shouted! Everyone in the class abruptly turned to look at me, I was still wearing the paper nose and I sat frozen gawking at the teacher, "WHAT IS THAT ON YOUR FACE?" she asked! I said it was nothing as I swiftly removed it! "STAND ON YOUR CHAIR NICOLA" she bellowed! As I stood there the hierarchy girl stared trying not to laugh, but this time it wasn't horrible, I had made her laugh. I stood for the rest of the lesson on my chair with a massive sense of relief and maybe just maybe things were coming to the end of a very lonely road.

In the weeks that followed the paper nose event things did start to get better for me and thankfully I managed to get through the rest of my school days with not too many trials.

11

Choices Choices!

Being a teenager can be an extremely tough journey for some it's a breeze, whilst for others it seems to be an impossible journey. Some make really naff choices!

Starting college for any teenager is an exciting prospect, you're allowed more freedom and treated more like an adult, there are more opportunities that open up to you and you can study the subjects you actually enjoy.

September arrived and I was fresh into college I had chosen and arranged. I was so looking forward to a fresh new start and ready to conquer the world of acting with a dream of ending up in a London musical drama!

There were some great characters in my class and I made friends very quickly! There was a girl called Ella who was a large girl, wore gothic kind of clothes and liked to tell everyone how amazing she was at Shakespeare. Then there was Sarah, she was also quite a large girl with round rosy cheeks who looked as though she should be on the film set as a welcoming mum who was always baking cakes. Then there was Jason a tall guy with dark curly hair, he spoke really well and came across as `quite the actor`.

I still had that underlying "please like me" need but somehow at college it felt different. We all got to know each other day by day and started to form our own little friendship groups, it was great. I found college life much better, I could wear my own clothes, go out at lunch time, drive myself to college, the tutors treated us more like grownups than school ever did and I embraced it. I loved my drama classes and quickly but surprisingly started to love Shakespeare plays. My normal day would consist of drama, dance, poetry and English lessons, most of them I got totally lost in, in a good way. English however I just got totally lost at!! My vision was to be in a position where I was ready to audition for Drama school in London and then audition for West End shows or television work. My heart was mostly in acting although I could sing and dance too. My strengths were being able to totally embrace characters; people fascinated me anyway so I was constantly practicing mimicking people's characteristics! I loved people and stepping into someone else for me was easy.

I wasn't seeing my dad much at all at this time in my life, mostly because I didn't really like who he was any more and I had started to become cold hearted towards him. My heart had started to turn away from him; I had taught myself that if I build a big wall around myself then I would be protected from any more pain. I vividly recall the very last blow that my Dad dealt me it was whilst I was at college. I had been given an opportunity to record a CD in a studio. I worked with a great musician called Simon who was a friend of the family at the time and we linked up with a producer called Luke. It was such good experience for me although I must say I felt very out of my depth. The guy I was working with was so musically gifted and me, I was just a girl who could sing but never knew what key I was singing in or what timing I was coming in on. I literally winged it, and did it all by ear however I absolutely loved every minute of it, then to hear it on an actual cd with all the music and the effects it really boosted my confidence. For the first time in ages I was really proud of myself and felt such a sense of achievement. I felt as though that hidden Nicky on the inside of me was being a tiny bit heard saying   "look what I have in me there's more too!!" I was beaming as I showed my Mum, Will and my sisters, it was a lovely moment. When all of the CD's were ready I was able to have few to give to friends and family, I decided to send one to my Dad, I thought it would be a proud moment for him too so I posted one to him the next day.

In the meantime, I had also auditioned for a well known drama school in London which I had arranged for myself through the college, so things were really looking up for me. I felt as though I was making tracks towards my dreams. I felt pumped and excited. I remember the morning the letter came through from the school in London. Mum came to my room and I held the letter in my hands nervously. Whilst opening it I also noticed mum was holding a package for me and I soon realised it had dads hand writing on it. Could this be the best day of my life; I get an acceptance into the school and my dad is sending me a letter to tell me finally how proud he is of me? I read the first letter with my heart beating a little faster than normal. I had been asked for a call back which was good news, but initially when I auditioned they didn't call out my name so this letter was confirming that I could come and re audition. It was something to think about but my mind was elsewhere as I considered what was inside the package my dad had sent me, I looked at mum standing over my bed as I ripped it open. My CD I sent my dad dropped out of the package and onto the bed, it had a letter with it too. I was confused, why would my dad send me my CD back? I read the letter and I was shocked. The letter explained that he had sent the CD back to me as he had read the acknowledgements on the back of the cover and he could not see his name anywhere and therefore he wanted nothing to do with it! I was dumbfounded. I looked at mum with tears in my eyes and then just broke down. Mum read the letter and looked so sad for me but so mad with him! For me that was it! The final shot, mum hugged me, I looked at her and said "That's it mum, he will never hurt me again and he is no longer a part of me or my life, I am done!" I wanted nothing more to do with my dad.

It was from that day onwards that that little piece of my heart that was supposed to be dedicated for my earthly father was now well and truly closed, out of bounds. I had made a pact with myself that neither he nor any other man would ever be allowed to access that part of me again. I would no longer allow myself to hope that my Charles Ingles dad would ever be a reality, my heart had been shot too many times and now it was closed. I was 17 years old.

12

The Maze

College was still exciting for me. I could now drive and rocked up to my new course in my gold Ford Fiesta given to me by mum and Will through my nan changing her car. It wasn't the coolest car on the road but for me it was a car none the less and independence, and for that I was grateful. I was still enjoying studying performing arts and it was a venture I was genuinely excited about. I had organised it and put everything into place before I had started so felt very mature for doing that. I enjoyed meeting more new fellow thespians and was getting to know more people. Our teacher at the time seemed like a good guy although I had to get past the hairdo he had which I can only explain as too long at the back with not enough on top if you get my drift. However I was settling into the course really well and found a few friends to hang out with.

At 17 I still wasn't sure of who I was or my values and definitely had no personal boundaries. In fact I didn't even know what a boundary was. I only recognised it as when a teacher would yell at us about not being allowed on the grass at school shouting "get off the grass you're out of bounds!" that was my boundary, the grass with white lines type.

Surprisingly however I got myself really organised for college, not like school at all. I knew what I had to do and when, and felt much more in charge of myself. I think that was due to being in my correct lane. My passion was acting and performing so for me I felt as though I fitted somehow, not with people but with acting and performing. I had made friends. I had a friend called Marissa who I was extremely close to. She was so encouraging and never came across as any kind of diva like some of the other girls, and she had the most beautiful twinkly blue eyes and a figure that most guys would check out, but more than that she was kind, a truly good friend. I still felt very much on the outskirts of people and groups though. I still found myself pedestaling certain people, normally girls that seemed as though they had it all together, body confident girls, girls that seemed so comfortable in their own skin and didn't care who did or didn't like them. I always seemed so focused on everyone else and not on the qualities that I had been given; I seemed to be vacant and loosing myself more and more. My belief system in those days was I'm fat; no one really fancies me I'm just that nice funny girl, I'll never get a boyfriend who will love me for me, I'm damaged goods and I battled HUGELY with rejection.

I started to hang out more and more with a few of the girls after college and for sleepovers. Some girls looking back now were so not my kind of people and I probably wasn't theirs but we were young and carefree and I started to make some really poor choices outside of college. We used to go out into London and hang around with dance groups that would do performances in the clubs and raves.

I don't really remember the first time I took drugs with them all but I think we were in a club. We started taking drugs most weekends in those days and I remember I started to want to go out and score more than just going out and having fun. I remember one night I scared myself as I had taken far too much and partied for a few days. I lost my care when I was out of it. I didn't care what people thought about me. I felt falsely good about myself. I used to be on a high, well, until I came back down again with a thud and I would always have reality waiting there for me. When I took them again I became the girl I thought I wanted to be. I had a false confidence that was fuelled by chemicals. I danced the way I wanted to and relished the attention I got. I was playing Russian roulette with my precious life but I simply did not see it.

I went on having crazy weekends with my friends and then back to college on a Monday morning. I seemed to manage keeping myself going during the week and still had a passion to act in whatever way I could. I would still practice my mimicking and acting techniques at home and go over my monologues ready for exams that we would be taking. I would get lost in stepping into a character and speaking their words with their voice, their outlook on things and the way they would stand or sit or pause before they would speak. I felt almost as though I would transform into the person I was being. I got lost in it because that was my gift, and although I was very unsure about a lot of things in those days about who I was, I knew very well and was very certain that I had a gift in acting and it was great release to be someone else.

My vision was still to either do some television work in a series or I would have loved to perform in a West End show however to get to that was a total maze to me. I remember imagining often that one day I'll be walking somewhere and I'll be spotted by a casting director because I'll be just right for the part in his series or film and I'll be whisked off and it will all happen and all fall into place, all my dreams will be fulfilled and I will tell my family and celebrate.

You see without realising it in those days I didn't understand process! I was always looking for the events in life yet I didn't understand that to get to those events you have to go` through` a process! I had already auditioned for a drama school in London and had had a recall letter, yet I had been more focused on the rejection letter from my dad than my recall letter from the drama school! I was still meditating on incorrect things and believing about myself those all too familiar` you're not worth it` thoughts. I didn't then understand about true self worth or validation of me as a young woman. I honestly believed that what was important was how much attention I got from the opposite sex, what my body looked like and what the mirror portrayed when I looked in it!

Achievement was my other thing. I thought my worth was connected to achievements. I would secretly think to myself that if I was to become super successful then that would prove to everyone how great I am! And then I would gain peoples belief in me! Not realising in those days that the problem was that I didn't respect myself.

You see I wasn't ever told by my dad that I was his Princess and that he would protect and guide me. I was never ever stamped with a daily validation that who I was was enough. I was never told that I was amazing or that he was so proud of me. I craved that, I was thirsty for it, yet my heart was now closed and I was hardened to it. Of course my worth got distorted and was placed in things that would water down and dull the gold that was in me, in worldly measurement of worth, I was becoming more and more a product of my environment and who I was spending the most time with. Broken girls attract broken girls.

Remember I had been told that I was going to be an abortion

and that I was never wanted. My dad said he only wanted two children. I was the third so of course I was confused about my worth and trying to find it in wrong things, why wouldn't I! I went with things that made me feel good, that got me that superficial attention. I became addicted to acceptance and approval! I had a deep need in me that wanted... no needed, to be loved.

13

The Turn Around

College came to an end and I received my NVQ in performing arts along with my LAMDA (London Academy of Dramatic Art) exams and medals. I was happy with that. Dad was now totally absent from my life and I had no contact with him at all, I had even changed my name to my step dad`s surname. I didn't think about him anymore I had stopped my head going there.

I was spending a lot of time with Marissa and we would have some very dangerous, crazy, fun risk taking nights out. I was seeing a really nice guy too who I had met in a club, nothing serious as I still had no clue about relationships.

I had tried various jobs to try and earn some money. Was still living at home and winging my way through work. I was working for an Estate Agency. Absolutely nothing to do with acting but was focused on getting a car so tried to find a job that would accommodate that! I would go out weekends, see my friend and see my sort of boyfriend! I would still trudge through life with this heaviness and sadness that I was a bit of a misfit; I would partner with anxiety on a daily basis and still play the clown to overcome it all. I had a truly turbulent relationship with myself and my mind was totally out of control. Thoughts about who I should be, how I should look, how thin I should be, will I ever be loved and understood, how I should act, how I should respond to people. I felt really lonely. I was self harming, not badly, but enough to help me feel the pain I was in. It was a physical pain I was inflicting on myself as I was angry and didn't know how to express it emotionally so by hurting me it released some of it through the feeling of the physical pain. That helped a bit but I knew I was dipping below the safety line. I had everything going for me yet my feet felt on really thin ground and I knew that soon I would lose my footing to life. I got incredibly low.

I was at work one day and something in me just gave up, I stood in the office and I was looking at a piece of paper that I had in my hand. I turned and said to my manager "I need to go home", he asked if I was ill, I told him that I wasn't but I needed to go home that instant. I had broken. My mum and now Step dad (my mum married Will when I was 11) came to pick me up and I went home. I was signed off work by my GP and I spent my days at home, vacant, I really did not care anymore. I had allowed all the pain and hurt and loss in my life to build up on the inside of me and I was done. I felt nothing.

My Auntie came to visit from Bristol. She was one of my favourites. When she was heading back she said to mum "Why don't I take Nicky with me for a while, it might do her good?" Mum agreed and I packed some things. We stayed at her little house that she moved into after the breakup of her marriage to my uncle it was small but cosy. I was smoking really heavily and living on very little food as i had no appetite, I don't know if I wanted to try and prove to everyone how sad I was by losing weight or I just felt so out of control that I tried to control my intake of food, I honestly don't know but I was in a sorry state. I remember having a dream one night about going to visit a previous boyfriend`s grave from when I was 15, (he had cancer and he knew he was dying and in our innocence we used to talk and say that if he did die that he would try and speak to me somehow!) My dream was me sitting by his grave and he put his arm out telling me he didn't like it.

   In the morning I sat up in bed thinking about him and feeling that pang of loss again. I made a decision. I`d had enough of life and I wanted out this time. That morning I sat in the bath contemplating how I would do it. I went through all of the options, I had convinced myself that this would be the easiest way out of all the pain, confusion and sadness that I felt and I couldn't see a better way to make it all stop! I sat for ages, staring and thinking about how to commit suicide, I felt strangely calm. I thought about a few things. I wondered how my auntie would get my body out of the bath and what she would do when she found me! Then I thought about my mum, step dad, sisters and my little brother and visualised how this would impact them and turn their lives upside down. I knew the decision I made would no longer be about me but it would be about the people that I most loved in this world!

   As though I had a sudden re think, I got out of the bath, dried myself and got dressed. I went into the lounge where my auntie was and asked her if she wanted anything from the local shop on the corner. She said no so I left the house and walked down the road I was in a calm yet surreal mood. At the end was a another road I had to cross to get to the shop opposite, without looking or thinking to look I walked across the road with no care if a car was coming or not. Strangely, that was what woke me up! I had got to a place in my head where I didn't care about me anymore, I was absent from myself I had let go of me.

   I went home, thin and quiet. I was taking anti depressants to try and lift my mood and sleeping pills to try and get some rest. I was resigned off by my doctor again from work. Thank goodness my mum and step dad Will were both so understanding as they had both had episodes in their own lives of the dark cloud that can descend over you. That was such a big relief to not be pressured to pick myself up and get better quicker than I was able. I really needed to be around people like that, people that didn't judge me or accuse me of being a drama queen. I couldn't have handled that. I needed time and space to get back onto my feet. I was in a space of what felt like nothingness. I was empty yet so full up at the same time. I was frozen yet moving extremely fast. I was present yet absent. I was at rock bottom. I only wanted to be alive because I didn't want to put my family through my death.

My turn around came whilst sitting in the kitchen one day. I was at the breakfast bar in silence and on my own. I was thinking about what I would do with my life. I was studying the walls, looking at pictures and little sayings that mum had up around the kitchen. My eyes stumbled upon a poem called "Footprints". I was familiar with this poem as I had seen it on the wall many times, I had even read it before, but when I read it this time it was as though it was speaking directly to my heart, penetrating through absolutely everything negative and shining light and hope into the depths of my very being. I sat surprised. I took notice of each word and sat there absorbing its truth. Then I started to weep, it was as though a rag had been gently removed from my eyes and I sat staring at a sun that I had not seen for a while. I took a deep breath and read it again. I heard this still small voice that I thought was me saying "you are no longer alone". I sensed this comfort blanket being placed around me, claiming me and carrying me. I felt numb but felt everything all at the same time. I felt found! I knew from that moment that my journey would be a journey that was no longer solo. I had a forever companion and although I knew there was a lot of work to do I sensed that somehow I would never be doing it alone again. I was 19 years old and my journey to getting well and restored had only just begun.

For you.

Knowing your value
You'll know your worth

Knowing your worth
You'll know your identity

Through finding your identity
You'll find your purpose

When you find your purpose
You'll know true love

When you know true love
You'll understand your value

Here is a little taster for the next book coming out in 2020...

`Renew and Be You`

I have walked this earth for over 44 years; I know I still have so much more to learn, but so far I have experienced many things and with the best help, overcome many things. I can hand on my heart say I am happy with who I am today and I believe I have a good future ahead of me. Challenges come and challenges go, but one thing that has always helped me is to remain in the day that I am in, embrace change, change hoped for and change unwanted, to be kind, even when it hurts, to love anyway no matter how deep you may have to dig, and to always remember to have an attitude of gratitude.

Chapter 1 - The Turn Around

I had just returned from Bristol where my knee jerk suicide plan did not `plan out` thank goodness. I had sensed this light and warmth through "footprints in the sand" poem, and something had shifted although I didn't fully understand what it was at the time, I just knew that I could trust it. I still felt exhausted but I also recognised that the only way for me now was up. I couldn't have gone any lower and death was no longer an option for me. I had this knowing that my change had to come from the top, my head! I had to think about what I was thinking about, what I was telling myself, what words I was listening to, what advice I was taking. I had to learn how to protect my heart.

www.ingramcontent.com/pod-product-compliance
Lightning Source LLC
Chambersburg PA
CBHW020430010526
44118CB00010B/511